Three Steps to Mindfulness

Bringing Zen Awareness Into Your Life

Kipp Ryodo Hawley

With great appreciation for my teacher,
Roshi Wendy Egyoku Nakao

Many thanks to Sensei John Daishin Buksbazen and
Gerry Grossman for proofreading and suggestions

Three Steps to Mindfulness

Introduction

What is mindfulness? How do we get it? What do we do with it once we have it?

Continuous, clear awareness of the present moment. Always returning, whether from an emotional outburst, an enjoyable fantasy or a melancholy remembrance; always returning to this moment. Rather than having your "mind full" of something, mindfulness clears out excess mental and emotional baggage, bringing clarity and a fluidity of mind that allows thoughts, feelings and perceptions to flow smoothly through without sticking and hindering each other.

How do we get it? Mindfulness is something you do rather than get. But, as you find as soon as you start trying, it can be quite difficult to simply pay attention to what is happening right in front of you. If you're like most people, you've trained yourself over many years to spend your energy following your inner narratives. So, as soon as you've set your awareness on something, it bounces away to interpretations, speculations and projections, often ending up in a swirl of emotion. To change this you have to re-train your mind.

What do we do with it? Mindfulness conditions your experience of the present moment, so it informs all your perceptions and actions. At heart is the opening of a quietly joyful awareness, but it can also be consciously applied to specific situations. When you're feeling stuck or overwhelmed, you can use mindfulness as a tool to help you regain your mental footing and resolve the problem.

∞

We each have our own ideas about mindfulness. And, there are many ways to practice it. Some are strictly technical, some are based on religious devotion. This book presents a new path to mindfulness based on the experience of unity of body, heart and mind that is fundamental to Zen.

Before looking into this new path, take some time to clarify your own view of mindfulness. What are your expectations? What do you want from it? Here are some ideas from those who have attended Three Steps workshops:

"Seeing what is."

"Open, focused awareness."

"Not zoned out."

"Present in the moment."

"Being in touch with life."

"Dissolution of the subject/object relationship."

"Freedom to observe and notice."

"Letting experience guide your mind, not the other way around."

"Conscious and aware of only what you are doing."

"A mysterious gate between Relative and Absolute."

Your viewpoint is absolutely unique. So, some of these replies may not resonate with you. At the deepest level, though, each of them seems to express our shared yearning for clarity of mind and action.

Zen

"Old Spring, New Water."

I heard this short poem recited by a young Japanese Zen monk at Zenshuji Temple in Los Angeles. It was the New Year's Day celebration, and he was marking it with his favorite poem. Zen poetry illuminates the larger issues of life by illustrating them with concrete, seemingly mundane things. Flowers on a hillside, the mist on a river in autumn, fish swimming freely through a stream – these images from Zen verses are windows into the awakened life, beckoning you to look through them.

In this case, it was a new year, a new day, and the young monk was beginning his new life as a priest. This is clearly "New Water". But what is this Old Spring? What is the Source? Short as it is, this poem can open up new worlds for us, simply by balancing our perspective, by showing us the underlying wholeness of life. The water is the spring, and the spring is the water, yet the spring is ancient and the water is bubbling new and fresh.

What is the poet trying to illustrate? You can view the water as representing all the constantly-changing details of your life – always flowing, continuously presenting new challenges and opportunities. Like each drop of water, each day is a new day, similar perhaps to earlier ones, but completely unique. The sun rises, so you wake from your dreams and launch your morning routine. But this morning there's a call from your supervisor saying you have to be at work early to handle an emergency. Quite different from yesterday, when nothing exciting happened at work. Yesterday and today are similar but different drops of New Water. Last night you had an argument with your life partner, but tonight you're going out to celebrate your anniversary.

Now, what about the spring? It is both the source and the sum of the water, producing and containing every drop and trickle. What could it represent? Here, every idea falls short. As soon as we imagine something, we've immediately excluded something else. We could say "The Universe", but even the vast picture conjured in the mind by that overused phrase is still only a picture, a tiny piece of the whole. We may intuitively feel an underlying wholeness of life, but experiencing this directly requires something other than the imagination. The quest for this direct experience is often the driving force behind those on the spiritual path, who say "I want to see the Truth for myself!"

We all see the droplets, the details of life. We put a great deal of time and effort into arranging them the way we want them to be, riding the rollercoaster of joy when things go our way and frustration when they don't. But we don't easily see the other side, the underlying unity of life. When we do experience it, whether through chance or as the fruit of a spiritual practice, we recognize the wholeness that has always been right there in front of us. This opens up a peaceful world, a world of no lack and no contention. This is the foundation of Zen – the world of no boundaries where equanimity of mind is found, appearing naturally the way the moon appears in the sky when the obscuring clouds are blown away.

∞

What would happen if we could clearly experience both sides? If we could integrate the world of no contention with our day-to-day world, the one that seems so hectic? What if we had a clear path leading to this integration? What if this was something we could do continuously, letting us return to clarity not just once, but moment after moment, especially when we feel overwhelmed? This is how Zen Mindfulness works, and practicing it allows us to accept each moment of our life as naturally as the Old Spring accepts each drop of New Water.

A New Way

The Three Step method is a roadmap to the mindful life.

Mindfulness is one of the fundamental tenets of Buddhism, and Zen Buddhists have developed unique ways of practicing it over the last 1500 years. Evolving in monasteries for much of its history, Zen life required the monks and nuns to pay continuous attention to detail throughout the day. From how they arranged their bowls during mealtimes to how they used the latrine, daily actions became rituals that required clarity of mind to perform. Continuing this evolution, modern Zen teachers create forms of practice for their students that draw on psychology, yoga, social activism and even baking to provide frameworks for the development of mindfulness.

Joining that stream, the Three Steps approach begins with treating our states of mind as places that we visit. We explore the landscape of each one and discover its characteristics so that we can pinpoint our position on the roadmap at any time. As we do this we learn to move between these mind states at will. Ultimately we see how to integrate and balance these states, moving from one to another to live our life in a dynamic way directly inspired by the living moment rather than being unconsciously driven by our fears, worries and fantasies. When we're emotionally overwhelmed, we recognize that we're in that "place" and remember to move down the path leading to equanimity. When we need to take resolute action, we know which mind-state is the best one for the job.

As we learn to recognize when we're in these mind states and move between them, we spend less time being "lost" – semi-consciously impelled from one emotionally-charged state to another – and more time being fully aware of our decisions and actions as well as the interplay of our thoughts and emotions. This is mindfulness built on the solid foundation of experience, so it is not easily shaken.

Zen Words

Since the Three Steps grew out of Zen, let's begin by looking into a number of quotes from Zen masters ancient and modern. Each is a glimpse into the spiritual mystery; each offers an entry point into the Zen world of no contention. Spend a few moments with each one, carefully considering what it means to you. If it means nothing at all, acknowledge that, too.

"Only don't know." – *Seung San Nim*

"You will see with the same eye as the ancient Zen masters." – *Master Mumon*

"Do you hear the sound of the stream outside? Enter Zen from there." – *Master Gensha*

"What is the holiest truth of Buddhism? Vast and clear, no holiness." – *Bodhidharma*

"Before enlightenment: chop wood, carry water. After enlightenment, chop wood, carry water." – *Traditional*

"Not two." – *Master Seng Ts'an*

"At first, mountains are mountains. Then mountains are not mountains, then mountains are completely mountains." – *Master Seigen*

"Cut off the mind road." – *Master Mumon*

"The Great Way knows no difficulties. Just avoid picking and choosing." – *Master Seng Ts'an*

Steps

The words of the great Zen masters reflect their profound realization of the Old Spring and the integration of it into their lives. A critical facet of the Three Steps to Mindfulness is finding that fundamental unity for ourselves. Now, this experience is so far from our usual view of the world that to get there we usually have to take a giant leap.

In ancient China, Zen monks and nuns would spend decades practicing silent meditation, grappling with their private demons, struggling to take this great leap to mental freedom. For this, they threw away their possessions as well as their attachments to family, status and worldly gain. Shaving their heads and wearing cast-off rags sewn into robes, they entered monasteries to devote their lives to seeking enlightenment. For some, the only instruction they would receive would be to simply sit with inner and outer silence – they were expected to discover for themselves how to do it. For all, the strict monastic discipline was a constant force stripping away their mental and physical habits down to the bare, clear awareness.

Finally, after endless hours of searching, of teetering on the edge of that vast chasm, they had become quiescent and ready for the great leap. Then, something quite ordinary but unexpected would happen – the sound of a bell, a thunderclap, or even a pebble striking a bamboo tree – and the world of unity suddenly opened up. What had been right in front of them the whole time was now perfectly obvious, and because of all those years of steady practice there would be no backtracking – they owned the experience unshakably. Having explored all avenues in the mind, they were fully aware of what the thinking mind can and can't do. So, staying in the realm of enlightenment became a clear choice they could make.

This really is the best way, because the experience rests on the firm foundation of years of practice. But what if, instead of spending years preparing to take the giant leap to Nirvana, you could break it up into a series of well-defined steps? What if these steps could bring you a glimpse of the fundamental Truth at the beginning of the process? How much time would you save, that you might otherwise spend groping in the dark?

Let me illustrate this with an incident from my own life. I was a musician living on the road in my early twenties. The life of the traveling musician has interesting parallels with the life of the wandering monk – each leaves home to become immersed in their way of life 24 hours a day, and each sets aside hours each day to practice. Of course, musicians are temporary wanderers, retaining a home base, and returning there after each tour, but even at home, music is their main focus.

At one point, I was the guitar player in a dance band based in Lake Tahoe, California. During a break from touring I was staying with one of my band mates, who had noticed how poor my diet was. He tried to help me by suggesting healthier alternatives from time to time. One day he offered me some yogurt, which I had never tasted before. Being open-minded I gave it a try, but it was just too sour for me to eat (in those days of the mid 1970's, commercially prepared yogurt wasn't as sweet as it is today).

Next he suggested I try some kefir, which at that time was often blended with various fruits. Kefir is also a fermented milk product, but its tartness was masked by the sweetness of the fruit, and I found it quite tasty. After a week or so of drinking kefir I tried yogurt again – this time I liked it. What was different? It was the same brand of yogurt that I had tried before, but once I was used to the small amount of sour flavor in the kefir, taking the next step to the sourness of the yogurt was easy – I no longer had to leap the uncrossable distance there. Now – what if we could make this kind of intermediate step toward mental clarity?

This is the key to the Three Steps. Instead of expecting ourselves to make the Giant Leap, which for most of us is simply not possible without the support of years of meditation experience, we break the process down to a series of steps. Like jumping from rock to rock to cross a wide stream, this lets us become comfortable with our progress after each step, and when it's time for the final leap it will be within reach.

The Realms

In the Three Steps method we view our states of mind as if they were geographical realms, each with its own terrain and landmarks. This is "where you're at", mentally and emotionally. For instance, when angry, our world might seem to be a steamy place bathed in red. Or, when peaceful, it may feel as if there is a cool clear breeze wafting through. Sometimes we're off wandering through old memories and sometimes we're sharply aware of our immediate surroundings. Each of these cases describes a realm on the Three Steps map. Each has identifying markers we'll learn to recognize and use to pinpoint its realm.

We all learn ways of navigating through our moods and automatic response mechanisms. We know when we're angry, and if we're lucky we'll see it early enough to stop us from being destructive. Or, we'll recognize when our mind is clear and decide to use the time productively. With the Three Steps, you'll be able to put your familiar mental pathways into a larger context and use them in a more conscious way. Now, you might say there are an infinite number of states the mind produces, but they tend to fall into a small number of broad categories. We'll be working with those categories, naming them and clearly defining their borders. Within those borders we'll find the rest of our mind states, almost like the provinces and counties lying within the boundaries of a nation. Just the way a paper map of Europe can help you find your way when exploring that continent, the Three Steps map of the mind will help you find your mental "position" at any given moment.

Once we've identified the realms we'll be able to "step" between them and learn to recognize the almost physical sensation of crossing their borders. Moving between them we also find that they have different characteristics when entered from different directions.

There is nothing wrong or right with any of these realms – we're simply learning to recognize the terrain of each, to know when we're there, and how to move from one to another at appropriate times.

Storyland

The first realm we'll look at is the easiest one to identify. This is where we seem to spend most of our time, where you may be at this moment. It's the subjective realm, the realm of evaluations, colorations and abstractions. For a quick snapshot of this realm, imagine you're in your local coffee shop, talking with your friends, laughing about the latest comedy you've seen or arguing about your favorite political causes. You're surrounded by the aroma of lattes, jazz music playing in the background and the light from the dim lamp over your table, but you aren't fully aware of them. You're riding the currents of emotion, but not fully aware of them either.

Now you have a picture of the realm called Storyland. We find our opinions here, our likes and dislikes, all our conclusions about the people and things in our life. There is a dreamy quality about this realm because emotion holds sway here. Looking around we find our hopes and fears for the future as well as our regrets and joyful memories of the past. This is also where we keep our stockpile of meanings as well as our "shoulds" – our strategies for dealing with difficult facets of our life. Included in this realm are all comparisons such as good and bad, useful and not useful, even hot and cold.

The overarching theme of this realm is our ongoing narrative about our relationships with the people and things in our life. We're constantly adding to it, embellishing it, re-weaving it, adding subchapters, looking for the moral. "Why did Joe have to say that hurtful thing to me? I can't trust him anymore." "Oh, there I go again, messing up my relationship with the people at work." "OK, this new plan of mine will make everything work out great." "What can I do about my sister? She's in trouble again, and just won't listen to what I tell her." These are some of the story lines we set up in our minds, and we buy into them completely.

When you are watching a good movie, you forget that you're sitting in the audience – you become completely enveloped in the story. Even more so when watching your own mind movies, except here there is no "The End".

When I'm reviewing the conversation I had earlier in the day with my boss, thinking I should have said such and such, I'm in Storyland. When I'm dreaming about how wonderful I'll feel after my next meditation retreat, I'm in Storyland. When I'm feeling the flush of anger and seeing red, I'm in Storyland. This realm includes all our plans as well as our obsessions, circular thinking and the endlessly-replayed mental vignettes known as tape loops. Maybe in this digital age a better analogy would be that of a portable video player stuck in shuffle mode.

This Storyland realm doesn't just include our inner narratives; it also includes our seemingly-instantaneous reactions to our surroundings. When you see a person, hear a bell, feel the texture of a piece of fabric, what are you aware of?

Let's take a look at some common things along with ways you might experience them in Storyland:

- ❖ Bell: "What a beautiful tone that bell has."
- ❖ Temperature: "It's hot in here!"
- ❖ Reading this book: "Hmmm, is this going to be useful for me?"
- ❖ Thoughts: "I just had the greatest idea about how to fix the budget problem!"
- ❖ Feelings: "Why did that damned traffic have to make me so late?"

In each of these cases, what you are aware of is your *reactions* to the objects in your immediate surroundings. This is the "stuff" of Storyland.

This Storyland realm can have multiple levels, beginning with evaluations of people and things, followed by stories built on the evaluations, followed by emotions generated by the stories. Each is like a layer built on the previous layer, and we seem to have a limitless capacity for adding layers – reacting to our emotions we add another layer of evaluation, weave another story around that, generate a more complex set of emotions, and on and on. The original facts of the particular situation may become completely buried.

When you reflect on this realm, what do you see? Two useful observations are that our stories frequently change and that different people have different stories for the same situations. This brings home an important point: *we create this realm and all of its contents ourselves.*

∞

Characteristics of Storyland:

- ❖ Subjective. What we're aware of is our evaluations and opinions of people and things.

- ❖ Emotional. Feelings aroused by our evaluations and opinions heavily influence our actions.

- ❖ Abstract. This is the stage upon which we play out the creations of our imagination. Our internal theater, thought laboratory and design studio all reside here.

Snapshot of Storyland: coffee shop conversation.

Orientation – the First Step

"Why do you stay in prison when the door is so wide open?"
– Rumi.

Now let's take the first of our Three Steps. Think of this as a backward step, backing away from something – stepping back out of Storyland into a new realm we'll call Orientation. Where Storyland is the *subjective* realm, Orientation is the *objective* realm.

You're not stepping back from Storyland because there is anything wrong with it. It's just that Storyland isn't the only mental realm; you're simply going to set it aside for the moment and explore another one.

This new realm is called "Orientation" because this is where you orient yourself in the world at the present moment, where you "come back to reality". Orientation is all about objects and their identifying characteristics without consideration of their value or relations with other objects. It's the realm of labels.

For a quick snapshot of this realm, imagine a laboratory with the technicians in white coats carefully testing their samples and collecting data. Everything is clinical, clear and concise.

In Orientation you're simply aware of the contents of your immediate surroundings, both physical and mental. If you are perceiving it *right now*, it is part of Orientation. If you can measure its size, weight or temperature, it is part of Orientation. The chair I'm sitting in, the computer I'm typing on, the jingle of someone's cell phone ringing – these are all found in this concrete realm called Orientation.

How do you take this step back? Think of Storyland as being an overlay. In the days before digital imaging, when you wanted to create a complex picture on a printing press you would begin with the foundation graphic on a piece of cardboard, then add type and other pieces of artwork by gluing them to clear plastic sheets called overlays. There could be several of these overlays, and they would be literally laid over each other to create the complete image. Then a picture would be taken of the compounded result, a thin metal plate would be etched using this picture, and finally the plate would be put on the press for the actual printing.

To take the step, mentally collect all of the Storyland material and put it on an overlay. Your opinion of the person you're talking to, the sense that you are late for an appointment, your regret about how you handled a situation last week – all your *feelings* and *conclusions* about things – these all go on. Now peel back that overlay, revealing what is underneath it – just the things themselves. This is Orientation. Spend some time here, simply seeing, hearing, smelling and touching your surroundings. See how each thing you are now perceiving in Orientation had been colored by the contents of the Storyland overlay, how some things had been completely obscured, while others had been given just a little tinge of meaning. When involved in Storyland you're quite unaware of many nearby things, especially those that haven't moved or changed recently. But now, in Orientation, you clearly see into all the corners of the room and hear all sounds, freely identifying all the objects of your perception.

When you take the backward step into Orientation, how does it feel for you? For me, it's something like stepping back through a bead curtain or out of an enveloping cloud – I feel an almost physical sensation of passing through the border between the two realms. You'll learn to recognize this sensation, like bumping over a threshold or clicking into a groove. I'm calling this a step back from involvement in Storyland, but it may help to think of it as a step forward, a step closer to "reality", moving forward through the overlay itself. Either way, what's important is the ability to recognize when you are in each realm, to peel back and replace that overlay, to freely step back and forth between the two.

Let's take another look at the common objects we visited in Storyland, and see how they appear in Orientation:

- ❖ Bell: "This is a sound that has been ringing for 7 seconds."
- ❖ Temperature: "Right now the temperature is 78 degrees."
- ❖ Reading this book: "I've read 1/3 of the way through."
- ❖ Thoughts: "I just had a thought about how to deal with the budget in tomorrow's meeting."
- ❖ Feelings: "I am feeling angry about the heavy traffic."

What is different about how these things appear in Orientation? Here, everything is concretely labeled or measured in a way that everyone would agree with. This is in contrast to Storyland, where others may well have a different interpretation from yours.

Once I attended the funeral for the mother of a long-time friend of mine. I had warm memories of my friend's mother, so I was in Storyland, wrapped in sadness at losing her. After the ceremony, I was talking with my friend and said, "This is a sad day." He then said, "No, this is a happy day!" He was remembering the suffering his mother went through before she died, and knew that death was a welcome release for her. We didn't have the same view of the event, yet we were both correctly describing our day because we were both in Storyland, and Storyland is always unique to us – we have created it in our own mind, so no one else can see it. Since it was time to move on, we both then naturally stepped back into Orientation and began talking about directions to the burial site and our plans for the day. Here we didn't have differing views because we were discussing concrete measurements of our surroundings – streets to take to the cemetery, how long it would take to get there, and where we would go afterwards.

Note that while we're considering thoughts and feelings to be part of Storyland, even they are phenomena that you can step back from and label. The thought that I'm careless for missing an appointment, the feeling of elation when something goes right, even the thought that I am thinking too much about how I feel when I think too much – each of these can be identified and labeled in the present moment even though their *content* is part of Storyland. It might help to think of the thoughts and feelings as containers that are carrying meaning, like cars in a freight train. Then you can see that the basic "stuff" they are made of – the containers themselves – can be clearly viewed in Orientation. Do you see the difference? That is where you find the boundary between Storyland and Orientation.

Practice – Labeling

Take a few minutes to explore this realm called Orientation. This is the land of names, so spend this time noticing and labeling things. Step back from Storyland and label the first thing that enters your awareness. The shadow in front of you is "shadow", a thought going through your head about your schedule tomorrow is "thought", the sensation of itching on your foot is "itch" – label it in a clear manner then let it go. When the next thing enters your awareness, label it then let it go. It's important here not to push these things away; simply let them drop like a toy from your open hand. Also, don't look for things to label; just wait for the awareness to arise then label it. Objects you see, sounds you hear, odors you smell, thoughts and feelings that arise – as soon as there is any perception, give it a label: "sore back", "bell ringing", "anger", "chilly" – no matter what you are aware of, give it a short, descriptive label. Do this practice for the next few minutes.

Now that you're familiar with Storyland and Orientation, take some time to write down your observations of how the people and things in your life appear in each realm. Give yourself a chance to get a clear grasp on the realms by taking two or three examples. For each one, first write down how it appears in Storyland, then write how it appears after stepping back into Orientation. For example:

"In Storyland, my work is full of exciting challenges and frustrating problems. My deadline is looming, but customers calling for technical support won't leave me alone. If there just weren't any customers, everything would be fine!

When I step back into Orientation, I see the computer sitting in front of me, a large photo of a French chateau on the wall, and a co-worker asking me if I could help a client on line 3. There are multiple trains of thought buzzing through my head."

Body Work

As you become aware of your surroundings, you also become more aware of your bodily sensations. Often, while in the throes of emotion, certain parts of your body will tighten up, such as the stomach, shoulders or chest. When you step back into Orientation, observe how these sensations change. Try taking a deep breath and letting it go in a long sigh as you take the step back. Are the tight places loosening up? Notice which parts of your body aren't relaxing and shine your awareness on them without judging. Are they connected to any particular emotion? Are they related to some memory or expectation you're replaying in your mind? See where the tightness leads you and get a clear picture of the story itself. Label the story and let it go while letting out a sigh and relaxing the clenched area.

There is a circular relationship between the story and the clenching – they feed each other. So, as an alternative to labeling the story and stepping back from it, try consciously relaxing the affected part of your body. Watch what happens to the story and its emotional grip on you.

As you get used to this process of stepping back from Storyland to Orientation you will appreciate more and more the fact we discovered in the chapter about the first realm: *you create Storyland yourself.* This is one of the keys to liberation.

∞

Characteristics of Orientation:

- ❖ *Objective.* Our awareness is of the physical characteristics of the things in our immediate surroundings.

- ❖ *Empirical.* We're involved simply in measuring and labeling each thing we perceive in a way that others would agree with, whether it's a nearby object, a thought or an emotion.

- ❖ *Concrete.* We are aware of the presence of things themselves without considering their meanings or ramifications. We're looking at the medium, not the message.

Snapshot of Orientation: technicians working in a laboratory.

∞

How many conflicts in our world today would simply disappear if the participants were able to step back from their individual Storylands?

Presence – the Second Step

"You know that space between your thoughts? Stay there." – Chogyam Trungpa Rinpoche

There is a place that I call Home. It's not the house I live in, but my house is in It. I keep wanting to return There, but I have never actually left. Whenever I return to It, I once again see that It has always been here.

In this vast "Here", everything is fully accepted, nothing is excluded. It's like a theater that presents comedies and tragedies – all appear on the same stage, and the stage doesn't discriminate between happy and sad stories, good writing or bad acting. All are accepted unconditionally.

This stage is our snapshot of the realm called Presence – the empty floor beneath all the dramas and comedies.

This is our original Home, the Place where we find all places and all times. It has always been right here, right now. With a little thought, we can form an understanding of this "Home", but it isn't really much help until we directly experience it for ourselves.

To do this, we'll take the second of our Three Steps, back from Orientation. Again, there is nothing wrong with Orientation – you're just leaving it aside to explore a third realm. And here's where your experience of visualizing the Storyland overlay becomes valuable – you'll use the same technique to peel back the layer of Orientation to reveal the realm of Presence.

First, step back from Storyland, releasing all your feelings, meanings and abstractions. Get clearly situated in Orientation – stay here a few moments until the fog of Storyland has dissipated and your surroundings are clearly in focus.

Next, gather up the contents of Orientation: all the labels and measurements, names, descriptions, locations, sensations of distance, even your sense of position within your surroundings – all these go on the next overlay. This should contain everything you are holding in your mind – all the outlines, names and distinctions of every kind, even those between the different realms. Any point of view, any lingering expectation, any idea of what should or should not be – put every bit of it on the overlay.

Let that overlay drop smoothly away, like a wave washing it off you, and simply float in the ocean of sensation. Now you are in Presence. This is the realm of immediacy. There are no memories here, no thoughts of the future, just pure perception without the mind clinging to it. When a particular experience is finished it's completely gone – no past, no future, just the crackling of the senses right now.

Presence is this moment itself, all by itself, this living moment that is the space every individual moment fills. Here there is no direction, no boundaries separating this from that, no measurements of time, simply the current of life buzzing through all our senses. This isn't a void or blankness, but the opposite – like electricity giving life to a light bulb, this is the stuff that gives life to all things, ideas, feelings, movement and non-movement. Nothing is excluded!

When you have let go of everything you are holding mentally and emotionally, Presence is what is left. You don't have to go anywhere to find it – you are already here, and have always been here. Your unique Storyland and Orientation realms obscure it, and when you let them drop Presence is revealed.

When you try to describe Presence, what problem do you immediately face? If you peel away the overlay containing the labels, how can you use words to describe your surroundings? How can you make distinctions between Presence and the other realms without immediately returning to Orientation? The answer is that you can use words and concepts to point to Presence, then leave those pointers behind and take the step. Immediately you find yourself in Presence, and you see that the words are no longer necessary.

Now you can see that just the way you create Storyland, you yourself also create Orientation. You decide the names and the ways to measure things. You are the creator of your own overlays, and you can decide when to remove them. You can also see now that *Presence is the one realm that you didn't create.* By peeling back the overlays containing Storyland and

Orientation, you see that the mental stuff you weave is what both orders and obscures Presence. This is Home, and it is always right here whether you are aware of it or not. Just as Storyland is the *subjective* realm and Orientation is the *objective* realm, Presence is the *essential* realm.

How would the common objects we described in Storyland and Orientation strike us in Presence?

- ❖ Bell: "Ching..."
- ❖ Temperature: "Whew!"
- ❖ Reading this book: "Hmmm"
- ❖ Thoughts: "Buzzzzz..."
- ❖ Feelings: "&@#%$!!!!"

Notice that for each of these examples, when you're in Presence, you're only aware of the bare sensation itself. You haven't distinguished it as being something apart from anything else, as something you're relating to, so you're not even aware of yourself as a separate entity; there is just the sound, the feeling or the sight that is occurring right now.

Practice – Just Sitting
Just as you learned to recognize the physical sensation of stepping through the border between Storyland and Orientation, now spend some time becoming familiar with the border between Orientation and Presence.

Sit in a comfortable upright position, take the step back into Orientation, and do the labeling practice until Storyland has faded away. Now point your awareness to the sensation of your breath going in and out through your nose and label it "breathing". Do this for three breaths. After the third breath, let go of Orientation and step back into Presence with a long sigh. Now just sit without putting your awareness on any particular sensation – let all perceptions flow through your awareness freely.

When I step across this border to Presence I feel my entire body and mind relaxing at once – I'm no longer holding on to anything either physically or mentally. It's critical to understand that this isn't a "kicking-back" kind of relaxation, which is a direct path to Storyland. Keep your back straight while letting all your other muscles relax, like a Zen monk sitting in meditation. In Presence we're fully alert with our attention tuned into the buzzing of this clear moment, and it's the mental and bodily clutching that we've relaxed.

Do this just-sitting practice for three minutes. If you can, set a timer so you don't have to watch the clock.

You will naturally find yourself straying away into Storyland, maybe immediately, maybe after a few moments. These side trips into Storyland are not a problem. When you find yourself there, simply step back into Orientation and do the labeling practice for three breaths. Then release into Presence and resume the just-sitting practice. Keep doing this until the three minutes have passed.

∞

Characteristics of Presence:

- ❖ *Immediate.* No past or future, just the crackling of life on the cutting edge of this moment.

- ❖ *Flowing.* Awareness of constant change in each of the senses, while not identifying them as senses.

- ❖ *Peaceful.* There are no boundaries separating things, no contention for space.

Snapshot of Presence: the empty stage before the play begins.

∞

In Presence our familiar distinctions between things like good and bad, here and there, and hot and cold are gone. There's no feeling that we have set them aside, or that we have somehow negated them – they simply aren't there. As the ancient sage Bodhidharma said, it's "vast and clear". There aren't even any distinctions of Holiness or Purity.

A Different Perspective

Now that you are familiar with the three realms, take a look at them from a different perspective. See them as being built upon each other like strata of earth or stories of a building. The essential realm, which we're calling Presence, is the foundation. It is the source or the container of the others, and there is no other realm behind or below it – this is the ultimate place where there are no distinctions such as separations between realms. The objective realm overlays the essential; it is the ordering of sensations into separate things. Finally, the subjective realm is on top – it contains all the meanings of the things in the objective realm and the interactions between them. Now – how would these realms appear if you approached them from Presence instead of Storyland?

Discovery

Moving forward from Presence, you cross the first border and find yourself in the objective realm, which we called Orientation in the first backward step. But now that you're entering it from the clean-slate of Presence, it's subtly different. Like the world at dawn, when the sun is shining on a new day, everything appears perfectly new and fresh; you see each thing clearly just for itself. Here you find the New Water in our short Zen poem. Since everything you perceive here is new, sharp, clear and free of previous interpretation, we'll call this realm Discovery. Here, just as in Orientation, you're aware of labels and measurements, proximity and distance. The difference is that you're opening out instead of withdrawing, so there is none of the overhang of Storyland fogging your awareness.

In Discovery, what do you see? What do you hear? Sensations are buzzing in all the senses, and you find them coalescing into a group of objects and events around you. You become aware of the ground beneath your feet, the song of the bird outside the window, the blood pumping through your veins.

This realm has the now-familiar sense of "place" you found in Orientation, and crossing the border into Discovery from Presence you feel the opposite sensation from when you stepped back over it into Presence: instead of the overlay feeling washed-off, it's now a sensation of putting-on, of acquiring. Here it's vital to remain aware that the objective realm is always created by you – you applied the labels and measurements to that overlay, which is simply a projection of your own mind.

Moving into Discovery you also become aware of other people and their individual viewpoints. You're not attaching meaning to any specific one, not even your own, so without preference or prejudice you can add their perspectives to the ingredients making up your current situation.

Resolution

Now that the things around you are clearly in focus, you become aware of relationships between them, and especially their relationships with you. These relationships acquire values – that bird's song is sweet, your heart is beating too fast, the temperature is a little too cold.

You have crossed the border into the subjective realm, perhaps without even realizing it. But again, just the way the objective realm had a cleaner aspect when entering it from Presence, the subjective realm you now find is vital and fresh. Here the values you attach to things and conclusions you reach are based on your situation as it is right now, so a sharp picture comes into focus. When seeing this snapshot of your world you experience a clear resolve, and if action is needed you find yourself taking it whole-heartedly.

This is a different experience of the subjective realm, so instead of calling it Storyland we'll call it Resolution.

Let's explore these new ways of viewing the realms by revisiting the common objects we described in the first two steps; how does our perception of them develop as we first encounter them in Presence then move forward through Discovery into Resolution?

- ❖ Bell:
  Presence: "Ching..."
  Discovery: "I hear a bell ringing."
  Resolution: "That bell has a beautiful, sweet tone."

- ❖ Temperature:
  Presence: "Whew!"
  Discovery: "I'm beginning to perspire."
  Resolution: "It sure is hot in here! Time to turn the heat down."

- ❖ Reading this book:
  Presence: "*Yawn*"
  Discovery: "I'm on the 25th page of this book and my eyelids are drooping."
  Resolution: "I'm too tired to read any more, so I'll put the book down and finish it tomorrow."

- ❖ Thoughts:
  Presence: "Buzzzzz..."
  Discovery: "There is a train of thought going through my head, giving me an almost physical feeling of elation."
  Resolution: "This budget idea is very good. I'll write it down clearly so I can present it at the meeting tomorrow."

- ❖ Feelings:
  Presence: "&@#%$!!!!"
  Discovery: "I'm feeling angry, and my stomach and chest are clenched."
  Resolution: "I'm overwhelmed with anger, and this isn't helping me get through this traffic, so I'll take a moment to breathe and relax."

In each of these cases, you're explicitly moving through the three phases that all your perceptions go through naturally: sensation, differentiation and valuation. The process is usually so fast that you may not even be aware of it happening: without seeing the perception and differentiation phases, you're only aware of how you value the event, so you immediately begin incorporating it into your stories without questioning it. But now you can begin to free yourself from this automatic process by clearly seeing your perceptions move through each phase and being fully involved in the final choices of value and meaning.

∞

For the next exercise, spend a few minutes observing objects in your surroundings, clearly experiencing the three phases of perception. Begin by taking the first two steps back into Presence, then rest there and simply observe how your perceptions form. Watch for when they cross the boundaries into differentiation and valuation.

Now spend some time watching how your thoughts arise. They may seem to spring fully formed into your awareness, and since they are complete they can be very convincing. But where do those thoughts come from? Follow their trail back to the source. See how they well up from the undercurrents of your mind and gradually crystallize into recognizable thoughts. At what point is it just a vague semi-conscious movement? When does it begin acquiring shape and feeling? When does it finally form words in your mind? The more aware you are of this process, the less you'll be unconsciously driven by it.

The process of explicitly beginning in Presence then moving forward through to Resolution can have a profound effect on your life, and this can be seen in the actions you take. The fundamental difference between actions taken from Storyland and those taken from Resolution is the source – Storyland-based actions clearly emanate from a localized spot within us and are typically driven by some fear or desire, while actions taken from Resolution seem to coalesce directly from the elements in our current situation and work to benefit everyone. Because of this, these actions fit the situation perfectly and feel almost effortless; it's as if the situation itself took the action, and you were simply an observer. People who are devoted to spiritual disciplines often report this phenomenon, and it's also familiar to those in the performing arts. They experience it while improvising or playing a part they know so well that they mentally step out of the way and the part or instrument seems to play itself.

∞

Characteristics of actions taken from Resolution:

- ❖ *Spontaneous.* Our actions arise from the situation as it is right now, not our ruminations about life in general.

- ❖ *Clean.* There is no emotional hangover because we don't make emotional investments in the outcomes of our actions.

- ❖ *Effective.* Actions taken from Resolution are the most appropriate because they spring from our immediate knowledge of the situation.

Integration – the Third Step

"To encounter the Absolute is not yet enlightenment."

This line from the Zen poem "The Identity of Relative and Absolute" launches us into the third step. This "Absolute" is called "Presence" in the Three Steps method. You have now encountered this essential realm, and have seen the other realms from two directions – stepping back from the old stories and stepping forward into life as it is right now. This is a static framework that you can use as a map to find yourself when you are overwhelmed or at a loss for how to respond to a particular situation. And now that you're familiar with the terrain of the three realms you'll realize that you're constantly moving between them, and have been doing so your entire life. But while up to this point you've been driven through the realms by your hidden desires and agendas, now you can consciously move through them as appropriate to current conditions.

Now, just sitting in Presence can be marvelously refreshing, since you're tuned in to the vibrancy of life itself. But eventually you find that it's not enough to sit there in raw Presence. The alarm rings, telling you it's time to get up and get ready for work. The baby cries, the driver behind you honks, a friend calls with an emergency, and you're brought back into the details of your ongoing life. It's time to take the third step.

Begin by clearly settling in Presence, deliberately using the first two steps. Then step forward into Discovery and clearly identify your current surroundings. What physical and mental objects are new? What new feelings and sensations are you experiencing? Which have disappeared? Which have changed? In what ways? Just the way a scientist carefully gathers data for an experiment, it's essential that your observations are clear and unclouded by your beliefs and opinions.

Next, deliberately move forward into Resolution, assigning values and relationships to the objects you identified in Discovery. In this situation, what are the important points? What are the strongest factors in any decision you must make? How do they balance and influence each other?

Finally, if the picture you completed in Resolution requires some action, take it wholeheartedly. It is clearly the most appropriate action, so you'll naturally take it without equivocating.

Now that you have taken the steps forward, formed a picture of the present moment and taken action, what happens next? You naturally begin analyzing your efforts, reviewing the situation to see what you can learn from it. You also update your internal picture of the people and things with which you're interacting, altering your view of them accordingly, and revising the roles you see them playing in your life.

What has just happened? You haven't crossed any borders, but Resolution has become Storyland. Often the transformation from Resolution to Storyland happens so fast that the values seem to be observations rather than judgments, and the judgment can completely replace the object itself in your awareness. As a defensive mechanism this process is crucial – you see a truck bearing down as you cross the road and immediately perceive danger, causing you to jump out of the way seemingly without thinking. But in different circumstances this instant evaluation can cause problems, such as when we come to a snap judgment about a person of a different race or religion from our own. In this case our actions will be based not on the person we're meeting, but on a set of generalizations we've collected about what we believe that person's culture to be. How would our actions appear to an impartial observer? Probably like we've lost touch with reality, since we're reacting not to the real person in front of us but to a picture we're holding in our mind.

We find ourselves back in our old home, Storyland. Our habit was to stay here, weaving and re-weaving our stories, wandering from one emotional pitfall to another, until some unexpected event brought us back to the present. But now that you've become familiar with the Three Steps realms you can use them – take the steps back to Presence and rest there instead of stewing in Storyland. What then? Move forward into Discovery and Resolution, take any needed actions, then return to Presence.

The Mindfulness Cycle

While the first two steps of this method are backward steps, the third takes us forward into an ongoing rhythm of living – of harmonizing with the world as it is right now. Thus, the third "step" is a continuous cycle through the three realms. This is the process of the third step, starting in Storyland:

1) Take the first step – back into Orientation. Anchor yourself clearly in your surroundings. This is the most critical step in the entire method, since it breaks the cycle of story-weaving.

2) Take the second step, back into Presence. Stay here for a few moments letting the overhang of the stories clear and your sense of position and surroundings fall away.

3) Now step forward into Discovery. Clearly look at your surroundings, your mental state, how your body feels. Here you see everything as brand new, as if you're seeing the world for the first time, and you do it without preferences or prejudices.

4) Take another step forward, this time into Resolution. Be fully aware as you evaluate the people and things around you. Pay attention to the relationships between them. You'll come to conclusions and contemplate actions that are based on the situation as it is right now: a subjective viewpoint with minimal coloring from your stories. If you now see an action that needs to be taken, do it wholeheartedly.

5) Watch the results of your actions as they unfold. You'll naturally begin digesting your conclusions and actions. But soon they're out of date – they're based on the world the way it was a few moments ago. Conditions have already changed, and you find that almost immediately these conclusions are transforming into new stories. Without taking any steps, you see Resolution turning into Storyland. So now it's time to let these stories go and…

6) Renew the cycle by returning to phase 1 and taking the steps back to Presence.

The Shift

In our habitual, un-mindful way of life, the time we spend in Presence is almost nonexistent. We spin around in Storyland, periodically making short trips into Discovery that are just long enough to take snapshots of how things are at the moment. Then we immediately return and weave the new elements of the scene into our ongoing stories. This often results in emotional churning, the digging up of old wounds and the re-ignition of pet peeves.

But as we practice this method, the amount of time we spend in each realm changes. We find ourselves spending more and more time in Presence, making short forays into the other realms as needed, each time dropping right back into Presence.

When you're spending most of your time in Presence your psychological center of gravity is low so you aren't fazed by events that might easily knock you over when you're stuck in Storyland. This is a momentous shift: you go from spending most of your time in Storyland, endlessly reviewing your mental tape loops, to spending most of your time in Presence, settled in the clarity of this living moment, our original home.

∞

Now we can clearly define our method of Zen Mindfulness: *the practice of making Presence our home and opening out into Discovery and Resolution to fit the moment.* Mindfulness isn't something you get, it's something you do.

Observations of practicing the Third Step:

❖ *When you realize you're in Storyland, that's the sign that you've been there too long. Regardless of the content!* Immediately step back into Orientation, even when in the midst of thinking through important matters. The salient points will still be evident, while non-essentials will dissolve away along with emotional baggage and other mental hindrances. This is the hard part, because of your emotional investment in your stories, but the more you do the process the smoother it gets.

❖ *The stories are the building blocks of ego.* When you identify with your stories instead of seeing them as transient phenomena that may or may not be useful, they solidify into the "small self", mental blockages build up, and problems ensue. Cycling through the realms helps break up the blockages and keep the current of your life flowing smoothly.

❖ *Mindfulness itself can be just another story.* When it's a goal you're striving for, a target in your mind or a memory you're trying to reproduce, it's simply another mind-movie that is distracting you from reality as it is right now. After working with the Three Steps, you can see how "mindfulness" can turn into a story that can trap you for years.

∞

There is no marking of time in Presence, so we could say it is older than Old. And, we can now see how all our actions well up from this boundless realm. Would the phrase "Old Spring" be a fitting, poetic name for it?

Results

This Zen Mindfulness is a way of seeing through the illusions we create for ourselves. The root benefit is the clarity of mind you cultivate by making Presence your home, and from this spring other practical benefits:

❖ *Equanimity.* The more time you spend in Presence the more stable your emotions become. Maintaining the continuous cycle through the realms gives you a fluidity of mind that lets you smoothly return from life's ups and downs instead of sticking there.

❖ *Direct experience.* After you've clearly experienced the objective and essential realms, your view of yourself rests on a foundation of knowledge rather than assumption and speculation. You *know* that the stories are created by you, you *know* that stepping back into Orientation breaks the story's hold on you, and you *know* that Presence is always there waiting for your return.

❖ *Effective action.* You're spending less time watching your internal movies, so you have more time and energy available to decide your actions and take them. Those actions are clear responses to your life as it is at the moment so they have the most impact while giving the most benefit to everyone concerned.

❖ *Relief when you're emotionally overwhelmed.* You learn to recognize when you're lost in Storyland and take the steps back out of it. When you've settled in Presence you can step forward into Discovery to clearly sort out the ingredients of the emotionally-charged situation and effectively work with them.

❖ *Time saved.* Instead of spending months or years sifting through your Storyland terrain looking for answers to your fundamental questions, you can categorize it all as Story-stuff, let it go, and move on to resolve those questions at the deepest level.

❖ *Insight.* The less time you spend playing with your stories, the more clearly you see That-Which-Is, "reality" as it actually is rather than as you think it is. The journey through Presence and Discovery to Resolution is at the root of many deep revelations, so making that journey yourself gives you a deeper understanding of the words and doings of the spiritual masters. And, by seeing how they map to the three realms, you have a clear framework for understanding those words.

Meditation

You have now learned to categorize your states of mind into essential, objective and subjective realms, and have seen how you can cycle through them to live mindfully. You've had glimpses of the underlying unity of life and have seen how returning to it can break your patterns of circular thinking and mulling over old stories. But, after practicing this method for a while, we can see how difficult it can be to maintain our cycle of mindfulness. And, we may wish to have a deeper experience of it – to see the Absolute more clearly, to more fully let go of our stories, to more clearly view our current situation in Discovery. What can we do to make this easier?

One way is to establish a consistent meditation practice. Among the benefits of meditation is the buildup of an inner strength of concentration, called *joriki* in Zen. This is the energy that we use to take the backward steps, and dedicated meditation builds it into a dynamic force strong enough to transform our life. This can make the difference between a tenuous step back from Storyland and a decisive one that leads us right to Presence.

If you haven't meditated before, it's best to learn from a qualified teacher who can help you avoid common pitfalls when starting out on the path. There are many facets to meditation, and an experienced teacher can help with your questions and concerns.

However, if you don't have access to a teacher, you can use a modified form of Zen meditation to help develop your *joriki*. Settle your body in a comfortable, upright sitting position. Make sure your back is straight. Next, take three long breaths, completely filling your lungs and completely emptying them during each breath. Then spend a minute relaxing your chest and abdomen and letting the breath fall to the pit of your belly. With each inhalation straighten your back just a little bit more, and with each exhalation relax the rest of your body a little bit more.

Once the body and breath are settled you're ready to settle the mind along with them. Take the first step back and do the labeling practice you learned in the chapter on Orientation. As each object, thought or feeling enters your awareness, give it a label then let it go. Do this for two or three minutes. After you're clearly situated in Orientation, make the sensation of your breath itself the object of awareness, labeling it "breathing" on each exhalation. Do this for three breaths then let go of the labeling while keeping your attention on your breath.

Now you are ready to begin your meditation. Maintain a relaxed yet sharp and clear awareness of the sensation of the breath itself. In Zen we keep this attention on the breath in the belly as it moves in and out, but you may wish to "watch" the breath as it goes in and out your nose. Let all your concerns go so that the breath completely fills your awareness.

The word "Zen" itself means "meditation" or "concentration". We concentrate not by tensing up, but by conserving our mental and emotional energies and putting them only into the object of our awareness. This lets that energy build, like water behind a dam.

As you're meditating you'll find yourself wandering off into Storyland. Once again, this is not a problem. Simply notice that you are in Storyland, then take the steps back to Presence and resume following your breath. Always return. It doesn't matter how often you drift off – what's important is to keep returning, over and over.

Begin by meditating for 5 minutes a day, at the same time each day if you can. When you find that you want to sit a little longer, go ahead and increase your time period by a few minutes. Do this until you're sitting for half an hour – after that it's best to break up your sitting periods, perhaps doing 15-20 minutes both morning and evening.

∞

Regardless of the style of meditation you do, I believe you will find your consistent meditation and your practice of the Three Steps throughout the day complementing and reinforcing each other quite nicely.

Specific ways to use the Three Steps

Moment-by-Moment Awareness
Maintain the rhythm of the third step throughout the day. This is the best use of the Three Steps method – deepening your mindfulness by continuously applying it to your everyday life. In addition, when there are breaks in your routine, take a few moments and explicitly do the first two steps, resting for several breaths in Presence. Then take the third step forward and resume the mindfulness cycle.

Emotional 911
Any time you feel overwhelmed during the day, take a moment to follow the steps to Presence. This is Home! Rest here a while then step forward and return to your activity. There is a saying – "Eight times down, nine times up." Every time you feel beaten down, return to Presence then step forward into the rhythm of the Third Step. This way, no matter how many times you fall you will still get up.

Meditation
We have seen how meditation can strengthen our mindfulness practice. Conversely, you can use the Three Steps to deepen your meditation. At the beginning of each meditation period, after settling into your physical posture, observe your state of mind and note the stories streaming through it. The content of Storyland is constantly changing, so use this opportunity to see its characteristics in the new details. Are you fooling yourself into believing the story? What's different about it that makes it harder for you to see through? Next, deliberately step back from the stories and do the labeling practice to get clearly settled in Orientation. Then take the second step and settle in Presence. Do the just-sitting practice for several moments then step forward and deliberately and clearly begin your meditation practice.

Whenever you find yourself in Storyland, do the Three Steps to return to your meditation.

Problem Solving
Deliberately choose to make your decision in Resolution rather than Storyland.

First, follow the steps to Presence. This clears the slate, removing the mind-clutter that clouds your thinking. Next, step forward into Discovery and clearly identify all the elements of the situation you're working with. When you've noted all objects and salient points, let the situational evaluations arise. These will carry you into Resolution. The picture that comes into focus may include an obvious action to take, several possible actions, or possibly none at all. If action is needed, but none of the alternatives is clearly the best, return to Presence and go through the process again.

It may take several cycles through this process to fully resolve the issue; each time through you'll drop off more leftover stories, sift out more inconsequential elements, and more clearly identify your action alternatives, so that eventually the most appropriate one is the only one remaining – then step forward and take action wholeheartedly. In poetic terms, this is action that is fully ripe, happening like a plum dropping from the tree at just the right moment.

Foundations

The Three Steps is a new way of looking at and using traditional Zen principles. Here are some of the specific teachings that influenced the development of this method.

Emptiness

One of the fundamentals of Mahayana Buddhism is the principle of Emptiness, or Sunyata. The central liturgy of Soto Zen, the Mahaprajnaparamita Heart Sutra, deals directly with Emptiness, and this piece is considered so important that it is chanted every day at Zen temples around the world. Emptiness is also at the heart of the Three Steps, where it is called "Presence". The emphasis on finding Emptiness and making it our home is what makes the Three Steps a Zen style of mindfulness.

Right Mindfulness

While Zen is popularly associated with enigmatic quotes and mystical depths of concentration, it draws from all the basic tenets of Buddhism. Especially important are Buddha's Four Noble Truths, the fourth of which is the Eightfold Path, the way out of our primal condition of suffering. The seventh part of this path is Right Mindfulness. The Three Steps extend the mindfulness-oriented elements of Zen, and are intended to give you a clear approach to moment-by-moment awareness whether you practice Zen or not.

The Three Worlds

In Zen literature, we sometimes find references to "The Three Worlds", the three domains of human existence. These are Desire, Form and No-form. While these aren't used the same way we use the realms in the Three-Step method, you can see that the Three Steps realms map closely to them: we are slaves to Desire in Storyland, we explore Form in Orientation, and No-form is what we find in Presence.

Karma

The word "karma" literally means "action" or "deed", even though we often use it to mean the results or retribution we get from our deeds. Bound up in karma is the intention behind our actions – when we act from greed, anger or ignorance we generate karmic seeds that eventually result in negative outcomes. Likewise, "good" karma gives us "good" results. But even these are considered unsatisfactory because all karma contributes to the turning of the wheel of Samsara, the endless cycle of birth-and-death. So, part of the practice of Zen is learning to cut the roots of karma.

In the Three Steps we train ourselves to let our actions coalesce in Resolution rather than Storyland. When this happens, we have no emotional investment in the outcome, so we are free to take action then leave it behind. This is the "traceless" action of Zen, and it is the kind that doesn't create karmic consequences.

Three Nens

These are the three moments of the arising of phenomena. The first Nen is the pure perception of something happening right in this instant, right now. This happens in the realm we're calling "Presence". An instant later we assign "something-ness" to the perception, distinguishing it from other objects around it. This is the second Nen, which brings us to that objectivity which includes both our realms of Orientation and Discovery. Another instant and we've given some positive or negative value to our newly-discovered object. Or, we may give it a neutral value, in which case our awareness of it typically fades very quickly. Here we enter the third Nen, the subjective, which in our method includes the realms of Resolution and Storyland. All of these Nens occur within a fraction of a second, and we're usually only aware of the third one because it continues on as we weave it into our current story.

Satipatthana Sutta

This discourse from the Majjhima Nikaya, one of the earliest collections of Buddhist teachings, is the Buddha's presentation of the foundations of mindfulness. It is considered one of the most important sutras because it presents what the Buddha calls the direct path to the realization of Nirvana. This path lies in the exhaustive contemplation of the body, feelings, mind and mind-objects. Within these four categories lie all the aspects of the self, and drawing from them the Buddha gives us an extensive list of specific items to use as our objects of awareness. For each, he says a monk practices mindfulness by understanding or discerning "I am breathing" when breathing, "I am sitting" when sitting, "I feel something pleasant," etc. This is the source of our labeling practice — in every case the practitioner is stepping backing into Orientation and thereby loosening their attachment to some specific part of themselves, especially the ones we don't want to consider.

In this sutra, the Buddha specifically emphasizes full awareness in all that we do. This is the ultimate aim of mindfulness practices, and maintaining the Cycle of Mindfulness is a way to cultivate this full awareness.

Three Zen Peacemaker Tenets

The Three Tenets of the Zen Peacemaker Sangha, founded by Roshi Bernie Glassman and his dharma successors, can be seen as guidelines for working with difficult situations. Originally developed to address conflict on all scales, from global war on down to our internal mental battles, the basic principles are also applicable to making the smallest everyday decisions.

As enumerated by the Zen Peacemaker Sangha, these tenets are "Not-Knowing, thereby giving up fixed ideas about ourselves and the universe, Bearing Witness to the joy and suffering of the world, and Loving Actions towards ourselves and others." Not-Knowing is settling into the clear mind, freeing it from all mental obstructions. Once we've done that we can Bear Witness, which is opening up to all sides of the situation without preference, putting ourselves in the shoes of all participants to understand their viewpoints. Once we've seen all sides we can move forward into Loving Action, to resolve the situation in a manner that works best for all involved.

Note that each of these Tenets is a verb. They can be seen as the actions we take in each of the realms as we move forward in the Third Step: Not-Knowing is what we do in Presence, Bearing Witness is how we open up to the world in Discovery, and Loving Action is what we naturally do when stepping forward into Resolution.

Questions and Answers

"I like being in Storyland. What's wrong with it?"
There is nothing wrong with Storyland or any of the other realms. But we can cause problems for ourselves and others when we cling to any particular one. When we get stuck in Storyland we act as if we had lost touch with reality. We can even be stuck in Presence – when this happens we can lose concern for our world and almost feel drugged. This is why we have the third step. Finding Presence is critical, and making it our home is the key to equanimity, but once we've done that we "return to the marketplace" and live intimately connected with our world.

You've seen people walking down the street, lost in Storyland, dragging their feet. When you're living in mindfulness, however, you walk with a joyful bounce to your step.

"I'm in Orientation, and I've measured the temperature as 'cold'. So now I get up and set the thermostat, right?"
In Orientation, there actually is no hot or cold. Mundane as they are, these are still value judgments, and while they may be valid, they belong in Resolution and Storyland. The most critical step is that first one back into the objective world – this is the beginning of liberation. And the more you practice it, the quicker you'll be able to separate the evaluations from the objects themselves.

"What about planning for the future? Isn't that Storyland? If I step back out of it, how can I get anything done?"
When we're making plans and decisions we're in the subjective realm, but in the area of Resolution rather than Storyland. When we approach planning from Presence and Discovery, we can avoid emotional trips and distractions that would otherwise cloud our thinking and even prevent us from coming to a conclusion. Then, once the plans are made, we can freely follow or modify them as needed because we haven't made a deep emotional investment in the outcome.

"How can I get my thoughts to stop while meditating?"
Each style of meditation has its own way of dealing with
thoughts. In Zen we're not interested in stopping the thinking,
just being free of it. How is this possible? By stepping back
from involvement with the thoughts. Use what you've learned
from the first step back to Orientation – this really is the key,
because it breaks the chain of causation leading to the tangled
knots of Storyland. Take that step back and label the thoughts as
they go through your awareness. View them as nothing more
than items you are aware of, like the sound of a car passing by.
This frees them to pass through and be gone. At that point, what
is your attitude toward the thoughts? If a thought is in your
mind, OK! If there is no thought in your mind, OK!

*"I feel that Orientation is unhuman – it's kind of cold and
forbidding."*
When you feel that way, which realm are you in? "Cold and
forbidding" is a value judgment landing you solidly in
Storyland. The idea of Orientation may feel unhuman, but when
you actually enter it you see that it is a completely natural, in
fact necessary, part of who you are. This question illustrates the
most difficult aspect of this method – our judgments can be so
deeply ingrained that we simply don't see them as something to
categorize, much less step back from. But again, this is the first
step to liberation, and the great benefit comes when we see
through our most closely-held assumptions and allow ourselves
to leave them behind in Storyland.

"This practice sure has a lot of rules!"
Look at these Three Steps as a tool in your spiritual toolkit.
Each tool requires a certain amount of training on your part to
master, and the quickest way is to learn the techniques that have
proved successful for others. Once you're fluent in the tool's
use you'll find your own ways of using it and will begin treating
the old "rules" as suggestions to be used or not depending on
the situation.

"How often do you use this method yourself?"
I personally use it every day, and seem to go through phases of using it for different situations. For instance, for several days I may spend my entire daily meditation time doing the Orientation labeling practice. Or I'll find myself practicing problem solving – clearing the slate by stepping back to Presence, opening up to what is true in this moment by stepping forward into Discovery, then clearly seeing the new relationships and making decisions in Resolution. Mindfulness is the result of practice, like the ability to play scales evenly on the piano. If we stop practicing, we get rusty!

"You said that in Orientation we measure things in a way that everyone would agree with, but I don't agree with my friend's measurements."
Remember that, although Orientation is the objective realm, we still create it ourselves. We decide the measurements and the labels, and someone else may well have different ones. Each of us is a unique viewpoint on our shared world, and even our own viewpoint is constantly changing. So, you are correct, we won't agree on everything we see in Orientation. Look at the spirit of it though – the point is to be able to step back into the place that is free of interpretation so we can free ourselves of the story-spinning.

"Why would I want to stop my melancholy remembrances?"
Mindfulness doesn't turn us into robots! We're humans, with emotions and memories. Part of our makeup is the constant interweaving of these memories with our perceptions of the present moment. And, swimming through the past can give us comfort and a respite from the demands of daily life. But when you become aware you are doing it, it's time to gently let it go and return. Always return! Indulging in these memories can be a kind of intoxication, a way to avoid your life, and at that point it becomes destructive.

"I can't seem to get my husband to let go of his stories and settle into the Now."

These Three Steps, and Zen Buddhism in general, don't depend on anyone else doing them. They are our personal practice, and we realize the benefits in our own lives. However, even though we don't expect anyone else to live this way, everyone around us does benefit from our own mindfulness practice. It's all about showing rather than telling or coercing. They will notice the results of your practice, and if they decide to do it themselves, fine. If not, that's OK too. When you are wanting someone else to take up some interest of yours, which realm are you in? Use this as another trigger that brings you back to awareness and settle back into the Cycle of Mindfulness.

"When I do the labeling practice, do I label my breathing and the labeling itself? It seems that stuff goes through my mind so fast I can't keep up with labeling each item."

It isn't necessary to label everything that comes into your awareness. One label every second or two is plenty. The point is to stay in Orientation by detaching from every perception that could start up the story-spinning. Here we can see how trying to keep up with the labeling can itself become another story. "I'm terrible at this – I can't even stick to labeling for more than 10 seconds!"

After you've done the labeling for a minute or two your mind will settle down and things will come into awareness at a regular pace.

"Identifying when I'm in which realm is kind of fun!"

This is part of the dance of Zen – we dance with life by zipping from one realm to another as the need arises, or simply to go exploring! The more time you spend identifying the realms the more adept you will become at slipping into the most useful one at any given time.

A Look Back

Now that you've learned the Three Steps and are familiar with the mind realms they lead us through, let's revisit the Zen words we considered at the beginning of this book.

"Only don't know."

"You will see with the same eye as the ancient Zen masters."

"Do you hear the sound of the stream outside? Enter Zen from there."

"What is the holiest truth of Buddhism? Vast and clear, no holiness."

"Before enlightenment: chop wood, carry water. After enlightenment, chop wood, carry water."

"Not two."

"At first, mountains are mountains. Then mountains are not mountains, then mountains are completely mountains."

"Cut off the mind road."

"The Great Way knows no difficulties. Just avoid picking and choosing."

Has learning the Three Steps helped clarify your view of these statements of the masters? Do you see them pointing to one or more of the Three Step realms? For instance, "mountains are mountains" might point to Storyland, "mountains are not mountains" might take us into the undifferentiated world of Presence, and "mountains are completely mountains" might be leading us into the fresh new realm of Discovery. How about "not two"? This clearly points to Presence, where there are no separations of any kind. Once we see that, it's an easy step to understanding the corollary saying: "not one, either".

The great teachers of Zen dedicate their lives to helping everyone wake up. One of the ways they do it is by giving us sayings like these, which we often find in those gem-like conundrums called koans. They are intended to short-circuit our story-weaving and force us to see reality with clear eyes.

"What is the holiest truth of Buddhism? Vast and clear, no holiness." How can this be? If there's nothing there, what's the point of it? Now you can see that "the point of it" is another story, and that "no holiness" points to the Holiness beyond holiness that we find in the infinite purity of Presence.

In Zen, "waking up" means awakening from the dreams of Storyland and opening up to the boundless possibilities of this vast and clear present moment. These sayings are not philosophical musings – they're descriptions of our life as it is and hints at ways to be fully aware of it. Use these hints. Let them lead you to the Great Way that knows no difficulties – the world of no contention – and you'll know for yourself the foundation of this Zen Mindfulness.

Parting Words

*"From the hundreds of times I lost the connection, I learn this:
Your fragrance brings me back."* – Rumi

The Three Steps method grew out of a talk I gave at the Zen
Center of Los Angeles in 2002, when the idea arose that we
could break our journey to the Absolute into a series of steps.
Investigating this further led to an afternoon workshop, which
was held several times over the next few years at ZCLA. That
grew into a full-day retreat, which is now offered once a year.
This book is an elaboration of the workshop, meant to be a
manual for learning and practicing the method. Thank you for
taking the time to read this little book, my offering of the
Dharma – I hope it benefits you and the others in your life. I
also hope that you got a glimpse of the Old Spring that is the
source of our life, and that these Three Steps will help you flow
easily with the New Water.

4319556

Made in the USA
Charleston, SC
31 December 2009